A Shakespeare Story

RETOLD BY ANDREW MATTHEWS
ILLUSTRATED BY TONY ROSS

ORCHARD

For Mum
A.M.

For Guy and Philippa
T.R.

ORCHARD BOOKS
338 Euston Road, London NW1 3BH
Orchard Books Australia
Hachette Children's Books
Level 17/207 Kent St, Sydney, NSW 2000
This text was first published in Great Britain in the form of a gift collection
called The Orchard Book of Shakespeare Stories, illustrated by
Angela Barrett in 2001.
This edition first published in hardback in Great Britain in 2002
First paperback publication in 2003
This slipcase edition published in 2013
Not for individual resale
Text © Andrew Matthews 2001
Illustrations © Tony Ross 2002
ISBN 978 1 40780 990 8
The rights of Andrew Matthews to be identified as the author and Tony Ross as
the illustrator of this work have been asserted by them in accordance with the
Copyright, Designs and Patents Act, 1988
A CIP catalogue record for this book is available from the British Library
Printed in China

Orchard Books is a division of Hachette Childrens Books,
an Hachette UK company.
www.hachette.co.uk

Contents

Cast List

The ghost of Hamlet's father

Hamlet

Son to the former King
Nephew to Claudius

Gertrude

Queen of Denmark
Mother to Hamlet

Horatio

Friend to Hamlet

Claudius

King of Denmark

Laertes

Son to Polonius

Ophelia

Daughter to Polonius

Polonius

Lord Chamberlain

A troop of travelling players

The Scene

Denmark in the thirteenth century.

5

Murder most foul, as in the best it is,
But this most foul, strange, and unnatural.

Ghost of Hamlet's father; I.v.

Hamlet

Snowflakes twirled in the wind that
moaned around the battlements. I turned
up the collar of my cloak against the cold,
and kept my eyes fixed on the place where
the guards had told me they had seen my
father's ghost.

Horatio, my oldest friend, was with me. It was Horatio who had brought me the news that my father, the king, was dead – bitten by a snake while he was sleeping in the orchard – and it was Horatio who had stood by my side at my father's funeral. Something in me died too that day, and was sealed up in the Royal Tomb with my father. My grief was so great that it sucked the light and joy out of everything.

From the courtyard below came the sound of drunken laughter.

"Someone is still celebrating the marriage of your mother and your uncle!" Horatio said.

He meant it as a joke, but the joke raised more black thoughts in my mind.

"How could she marry so soon after the funeral?" I said. "How could she forget my father so quickly?"

"You should be happy for her, my lord Hamlet," said Horatio. "She has found new happiness in the midst of sorrow, and your uncle, Claudius, will rule Denmark wisely until you come of age."

I laughed bitterly. I had seen cunning in Claudius's face, but no wisdom. I was about to say so, when midnight began to ring out from the turret above our heads.

And as the last stroke throbbed through the air, the darkness and the falling snow shaped themselves into the spirit of my father, beckoning to me.

Horatio gasped out a warning, but I paid no attention. I ran through the dancing flakes, my heart beating so fast that I thought it would burst. The ghost was dressed in armour, a circlet of gold gleaming against the black iron of its helm. Its face was my father's face, but twisted in agony, its eyes burning like cold, blue flames. Its voice was a groan of despair that sent shudders down my backbone.

"Hamlet, my son! My spirit cannot find rest until my murder has been avenged."

"Murder?" I cried.

"The serpent who stung me in the orchard was my brother, Claudius," said the ghost. "As I lay asleep, it was he who crept to my side and poured poison in my ear. Claudius took my life, my throne and now my wife. Avenge me, Hamlet!"

Before I could say more, the ghost faded into snowy blackness, and the echoes of its voice became the whistling of the wind.

My mind reeled. Had I really spoken to the ghost of my father, or was it a devil from Hell, sent to trick me into doing evil? I had suspected that Claudius might have had something to do with my father's death, but could I trust the word of a vision from beyond the grave? How could I be sure of the truth? How could I, the Prince of Denmark, not yet twenty years' old, avenge the death of a king?

I turned, and stumbled back to Horatio. His face was grey and he quivered with fear. "Such sights are enough to drive a man mad!" he whispered.

I laughed then, long and hard, because Horatio had unwittingly provided me with an answer.

Who could have more freedom than a mad prince? If I pretended to be mad, I could say whatever I wished and search for the truth without arousing Claudius's suspicion.

And so my plan took shape. I wore nothing but black. I wandered through the castle, weeping and sighing, seeking out shadowy places to brood. If anyone spoke to me, I answered with the first wild nonsense that came into my head, and all the time I watched Claudius, looking for the slightest sign of guilt. I cut myself off from all friends – except Horatio; I told him everything, for I knew he was the only one I could trust.

A rumour began
to spread through
the castle that grief
had turned my wits.
So far, my plan was
a success, but it is
one thing to invent a
plan, and another thing to
carry it through. The strain of pretending,
of cutting myself off from kindness and
good company, was almost too great to
bear. There were times when I thought I
truly had gone mad, when I felt I could no
longer carry the burden of what the ghost
had told me. If I avenged my father, my
mother's new husband would be revealed
as a murderer, and her happiness would
be shattered; if I did not, my father's soul
was doomed to eternal torment.

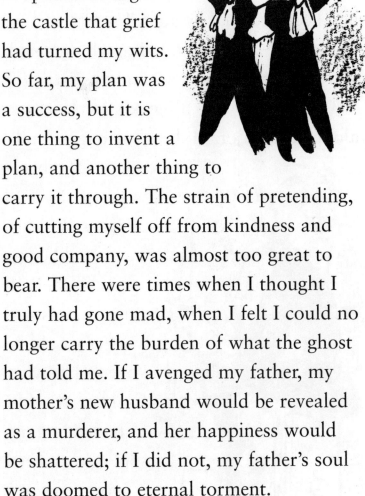

Worst of all, I was tortured by doubt. What if Claudius were innocent? What if I had been deceived by an evil spirit? Questions went spinning through my mind, like the stars spinning around the Earth.

Then one day, on a bleak afternoon, alone in my room, I drew my dagger and stared at it. The blade was sharp: if I used it on myself, death would come quickly, and all my doubts and worries would be over – but what then? Would I be sending my soul into an even worse torture?

I weighed the dagger in my hand, balancing the fear of what I must do to avenge my father against the fear of what might follow death. It seemed I lacked both the courage to go on with my life, and the courage to end it.

Hearing a knock at my door, I sheathed the dagger and called out, "Come in!" almost relieved at the interruption.

A woman entered. It was Lady Ophelia, her fair hair shining like a candle-flame, her eyes filled with love and concern.

My heart lifted, then sank. Ophelia and I had loved each other since we were children. Before my father's death, I had been certain that she was the one I would marry – but now everything had changed. There was no room in my heart for love.

"Lord Hamlet?" Ophelia said. "My father asks if you will attend the performance of the Royal Players tonight?"

As soon as she mentioned her father, I knew what was happening. Her father was Polonius, the Royal Chamberlain, a meddling fool who loved gossip and secrets. He had sent Ophelia to try and discover why I was acting so strangely. Ophelia would report everything I said to Polonius, and he would report it to Claudius. I was sickened: the castle of Elsinore was a place where brothers murdered brothers, wives forgot their husbands, and fathers used their daughters as spies.

I laughed carelessly, to hide the ache I felt when I looked at Ophelia's beautiful face. "Tell Lord Polonius that I shall be at the play," I said.

Ophelia turned her head, and I saw a tear fall across her cheek. "My lord," she murmured, "why do you never look at me the way you used to? There was a time when I believed you loved me, and wished us to marry, but now you seem so cold..."

I longed to tell her how much I loved her, and that my coldness was nothing more than acting, but I did not dare.

"*You*, marry me?" I said roughly. "Marry no one, Ophelia! Wives and husbands are all cheats and liars. It would be better for you to join a convent and become a nun!"

At this she ran from the room, her sobs echoing through the corridor, making my heart break.

And then, just as I thought there was no end to my despair, an idea came – first a glimmer, then a gleam, then a burst of light brighter than the sun.

I hurried from my room and went to the Great Hall, where the actors were setting up their stage. I found their leader, a tall man with a look of my uncle about him. After chatting for a few moments, I said casually, "Do you know the play *The Murder of Gonzago*?" "Certainly, my lord!" came the reply.

I handed the man a purse filled with gold. "Act it tonight," I said. "But I want you to make some changes to the story. Listen carefully…"

I meant to turn the play from an entertainment into a trap – a trap to catch a King.

That evening, while the audience watched the stage, I watched Claudius. At first he showed little interest in the story, preferring to whisper to my mother and kiss her fingers in a way that filled me with loathing – but gradually the skill of the players won his attention.

At the end of the first scene, exactly according to my instructions, the actor playing Duke Gonzago lay down as though asleep and his nephew Lucianus – played by the actor who resembled Claudius – crept up on him and poured poison into his ear.

Even though the light in the hall was dim, I could see the deathly pallor of Claudius's face as he watched this scene. His eyes grew troubled, and he raised a trembling hand towards the stage.

I knew then that I was gazing at the face of a murderer, and that everything the ghost had told me was true.

"No!" Claudius cried out, springing to his feet. "Lights! Bring more lights!"

But all the torches in the world would not light the darkness in his mind. His nerve failed and he hurried from the hall.

Mother made to follow him, but I stopped her at the door. "Do not delay me. I must go to the King!" she said. "Something is wrong."

"And I know what," I told her. "I must talk to you. I will come to your room in an hour. Make sure you are alone, and tell no one of our meeting."

* * *

But I underestimated Claudius's cunning, and the power he had over my mother. When she let me into her room, there was a coldness in her expression and I guessed that she had been speaking to my uncle. Before I could say a word, she said, "Hamlet, you have deeply offended your royal stepfather."

"And you have offended my dead father," I replied.

Mother frowned at me, puzzled. "What do you mean?" she demanded.

"You offended him the day you abandoned your mourning robes in exchange for a wedding gown," I said. "The day you married a liar and a murderer!"

"I won't listen!" Mother shouted. She began to cover her ears with her hands and I caught hold of her wrists to prevent her – she had to hear the truth. Mother screamed in alarm, and then I heard a voice from behind the drawn curtains at her window, calling out, "Help! Murder!"

I was certain it was Claudius – who else would skulk and spy in my mother's bedroom? I drew my sword and plunged it into the curtain, filled with fierce joy that my father was avenged at last...

But it was the body of Lord Polonius that tumbled into the room; I had killed an innocent man.

"You meddling old fool!" I groaned. "What were you doing there?"

"Following my orders," said a voice.

I turned and saw Claudius in the doorway, with two armed guards. A triumphant light glinted in his eyes. "I was afraid you might harm your mother if you were alone with her," Claudius went on.

"Your madness has made you violent,
Hamlet. You must leave Denmark tonight.
I shall send you to friends in England,
who will care for you until you are back
in your right mind. Guards, take the
Prince away!"

Neither my mother nor the guards saw the mocking smile that flickered on his lips, but as soon as I saw it, I knew that Claudius intended me never to return from England. I would be imprisoned, and then secretly murdered.

While I had been trying to trap my uncle, he had been setting a trap for me, and now it had snapped shut.

* * *

They bundled me into a windowless
carriage and locked the doors and I
was driven speedily through the night.

I could see nothing, and could hear only
the rattling of the wheels and the cracking
of the driver's whip, keeping the horses at
full gallop.

After several hours, the carriage arrived at a port, and I was placed on a ship that set sail almost as soon as I was aboard. I made no attempt to escape. It was all over: my father was unavenged, Claudius had outwitted me, and I was as good as dead.

Just before dawn broke, my life seemed to become some strange dream, for the most unlikely thing happened: I was rescued by Danish pirates. They captured the ship and murdered most of the crew, but when they discovered who I was, panic seized them. Fearing that they would be hunted down by the Danish fleet, the pirates sailed back to Denmark and put me ashore at a little fishing village.

There I found lodgings and wrote letters to Horatio, and to my mother. I told her that I would return to Elsinore and right all the wrongs that had been done – though I did not tell her what those wrongs were.

The next day, I bought a horse and set off, certain that Fate had returned me to Denmark to complete my revenge. There was no more doubt in my mind – Claudius was guilty, and I would make him answer for his crime.

I was still some way from the castle when I was met by Horatio, who had ridden out to find me. There was a darkness in my friend's face, and I knew he was the bearer of ill tidings.

"My lord," he said, "the Lady Ophelia is dead. Claudius told her that you had killed her father, and the grief drove her so mad that she drowned herself."

Tears blurred my sight. What had I done to my beloved Ophelia! In another time and place, our love might have grown into happiness...

"Ophelia's brother, Laertes, has sworn to kill you for the deaths of his father and sister," Horatio went on, "but Claudius persuaded Laertes to settle his differences with you in a fencing match, in front of the whole court. I have seen the King whispering to Laertes in private, and I am sure they are plotting against you. Turn back, my lord! Escape while you can to somewhere you will be safe!"

"No, I must go to Elsinore," I told him. "My destiny awaits me there. We cannot escape our destinies, Horatio, we can only be ready for them, and I am ready."

* * *

And so the ghost, Claudius, the pirates and
my destiny have brought me back, to the
torch-light and candles of the Great Hall at
Elsinore. Courtiers and nobles chatter idly
and make wagers on the outcome of the

duel. There, on the royal thrones, sit my uncle and my mother. She smiles at me and looks proud; he is anxious, and keeps glancing slyly at Laertes. Laertes is filled with a cold hatred that makes his eyes shine like moonlight on ice.

Horatio takes my cloak and hands me a rapier. His face is pale and worried. He leans close and whispers, "Have a care, my lord! There is death in Laertes' look."

I smile: death is everywhere in the castle of Elsinore tonight, and I can feel my father's spirit hovering over me. Claudius raises his right arm. "Let the contest begin!" he commands.

The blades of our rapiers snick and squeal. Our shadows, made huge and menacing by the torches, flicker on the walls as we duck and dodge. Laertes is a skilled swordsman, but rage and hate have made him clumsy. He drops his guard to strike at me, I flick my wrist, and the point of my rapier catches his arm.

One of the marshals shouts, "A hit! First hit to Prince Hamlet!"

Laertes bows, his forehead slick with sweat. "Let us take a cup of wine and catch our breath, my lord," he says.

The wine cups are on a table near the thrones. Laertes and I step towards them, and my mother suddenly snatches up one of the cups. "A toast, to honour my beloved son!" she announces.

"No!" hisses Claudius. He reaches out as if to dash the cup from my mother's lips, but he is too late: she has drunk the wine down to the dregs.

There is just time for me to see a look of horror on Claudius's face, and then, without warning, Laertes wheels around and slashes at me with his sword. I parry the blow, realising that this is no longer a contest – I am fighting for my life.

I see Laertes' eyes, blind with fury. I watch his mouth twist itself into an ugly snarl. He clutches at me and tries to stab under my arm, but I catch the sword in my left hand and I wrench it from his grasp. A pain like fire burns against my palm, and my fingers are wet with blood.

I step back, throw Laertes my rapier and take his in my right hand. *"En garde!"* I say.

We fight on, but something is wrong. Laertes looks terrified, and his breath comes in sobs. The pain in my hand is fierce, throbbing up into my forearm – I have suffered from sword-cuts before, but none as painful as this.

Laertes lunges desperately at me, and the point of my sword scratches through his shirt; a spurt of red stains the whiteness of the linen.

Laertes reels back. "We are dead men!"
he groans. "The King spread poison on
the blade – the same poison that he
poured into your wine cup!"

I see all now. I understand the hot
agony that is creeping through my left
arm and across my chest.

Laertes cries out, "The King is a murderer!" and crumples to the floor. At the same time, my mother screams and topples from her throne.

There is no time left. I must act quickly, before the pain reaches my heart. I stagger towards Claudius and he cringes in his throne, covering his face with his hands.

"Traitor!" I say, and drive the poisoned sword deep into his heart.

Voices shout...people are running. I fall back, and someone catches me. I think it is Horatio, but I cannot see him clearly, for a darkness is falling before my eyes...coming down like the snow falling, that night on the battlements...

Through the darkness, I seem to see a light...and my father's face...and everything drops away behind me...

Horatio's voice whispers, "Farewell, sweet Prince!"

And the rest is silence.

There's a divinity that shapes our ends,
Rough-hew them how we will.

Hamlet; V.ii.

Revenge in Hamlet

In *Hamlet*, Shakespeare portrays a young man who has been educated to be a thinker, but who becomes a man of action, motivated by the dark force of revenge.

When Hamlet discovers from his father's ghost that the old king's death was not an accident but murder, he is torn in two. The ghost claims that the murderer is Claudius, his own brother, who has recently married Hamlet's mother. Is the ghost telling the truth, or is it a demon sent from hell to tempt the prince into an evil act? Hamlet is left confused and constantly tortured by doubt. He can't decide what to do.

In a desperate attempt to uncover the truth, Hamlet pretends to be mad. He kills Polonius by mistake, and this leads to the accidental death of

Ophelia, with whom Hamlet was once in love.

In a thrilling climax, Hamlet agrees to a fencing match with Laertes. Laertes, having lost his father and sister, is full of despair and desire for his own revenge. He fights with a poisoned sword given to him by Claudius, who suspects that Hamlet knows too much.

In Elizabethan times, this final scene of *Hamlet* would have been full of spectacularly gory visual effects. To make sword-fights seem more realistic, pigs' bladders filled with blood were hidden in the actors' costumes, and pierced with the point of a sword or dagger.

The audience would have been spellbound by the dark tale of revenge, where a prince succeeds in avenging his father's death – but at a terrible cost.

Shakespeare and the Globe Theatre

Some of Shakespeare's most famous plays were first performed at the Globe Theatre, which was built on the South Bank of the River Thames in 1599.

Going to the Globe was a different experience from going to the theatre today. The building was roughly circular in shape, but with flat sides: a little like a doughnut crossed with a fifty-pence piece. Because the Globe was an open-air theatre, plays were only put on during daylight hours in spring and summer. People paid a penny to stand in the central space and watch a play, and this part of the audience became known as 'the groundlings' because they stood on the ground. A place in the tiers of seating beneath the thatched roof, where there was a slightly better view and less chance of being rained on, cost extra.

The Elizabethans did not bath very often and the audiences at the Globe were smelly. Fine ladies and gentlemen in the more expensive seats sniffed perfume and bags of sweetly-scented herbs to cover the stink rising from the groundlings.

There were no actresses on the stage; all the female characters in Shakespeare's plays would have been acted by boys, wearing wigs and make-up. Audiences were not well-behaved. People clapped and cheered when their favourite actors came on stage; bad actors were jeered at and sometimes pelted with whatever came to hand.

Most Londoners worked hard to make a living and in their precious free time they liked to be entertained. Shakespeare understood the magic of the theatre so well that today, almost four hundred years after his death, his plays still cast a spell over the thousands of people that go to see them.

Orchard Classics
Shakespeare Stories

RETOLD BY ANDREW MATTHEWS

ILLUSTRATED BY TONY ROSS

Orchard Books are available from all good bookshops.